The Bizarre Origins of Kangaroo Court
and Other Idioms

by Arnold Ringstad • illustrated by Dan McGeehan

Published by The Child's World®
1980 Lookout Drive • Mankato, MN 56003-1705
800-599-READ • www.childsworld.com

Acknowledgments
The Child's World®: Mary Berendes, Publishing Director
The Design Lab: Design and production
Red Line Editorial: Editorial direction

Design elements: Kirsty Pargeter/iStockphoto

ISBN 9781614732310
LCCN 2012932807

Printed in the United States of America
Mankato, MN
July 2012
PA02118

Contents

BEHIND THE EIGHT BALL

MEANING: A person who is **behind the eight ball** is in a difficult position.

ORIGIN: In the game of billiards, a player has to hit the eight ball last. If your ball is behind the eight ball, you have to hit around it, making the shot harder.

EXAMPLE: Dora was **behind the eight ball**. She forgot to bring her lucky bowling shoes to the big game.

NO SPRING CHICKEN

MEANING: Someone who is old and not active is **no spring chicken**.

ORIGIN: A spring chicken is a young chicken.

EXAMPLE: Doug's grandmother couldn't play tag with him anymore. "I can't run so fast," she said. "I'm **no spring chicken**."

BITE THE BULLET

MEANING: To **bite the bullet** is to face a bad situation bravely.

ORIGIN: This phrase comes from the time before doctors knew how to put people to sleep during surgery. When a soldier got hurt, a doctor would instead give him a bullet to bite down on.

EXAMPLE: Dexter had to **bite the bullet**. He forgot to study for his French test, but now he had to take it.

BALLPARK FIGURE

MEANING: A **ballpark figure** is a rough guess at something.

ORIGIN: This phrase is related to another idiom, "in the ballpark." Both use the concept of being in the general area (the "ballpark") without being exactly right.

EXAMPLE: Helga couldn't count the stars in the sky, so she wrote down a **ballpark figure**.

EXTEND AN OLIVE BRANCH

MEANING: Someone who **extends an olive branch** is asking for peace.

ORIGIN: In the Bible story of Noah's Ark, a dove carrying an olive branch signaled the end of a major flood.

EXAMPLE: Eddy **extended an olive branch** to Patti. He didn't get mad even though she broke his microscope.

ACCORDING TO HOYLE

MEANING: Something that goes **according to Hoyle** goes according to plan or follows the rules.

ORIGIN: A man named Edmond Hoyle wrote books about card game rules in the 1700s.

EXAMPLE: If everything went **according to Hoyle**, Miguel would save enough money to buy a new toaster.

PUT A SOCK IN IT

MEANING: When someone says "**Put a sock in it**," they mean "Stop talking."

ORIGIN: The origin of this phrase is uncertain. The likeliest explanation is that it was started by British and Australian soldiers in World War I. The meaning comes from the idea of putting a sock in someone's mouth to quiet them down.

EXAMPLE: "**Put a sock in it**!" Suzy whispered to the people talking loudly in the library.

BATTING A THOUSAND

MEANING: A person who is **batting a thousand** is successful every time.

ORIGIN: In baseball, a player's batting average shows how often he or she gets a hit. The average is written out with three decimal places. A player who gets a hit half the time bats .500. A player who gets a hit every time bats 1.000, which looks like one thousand.

EXAMPLE: Carl was **batting a thousand**. Every time he wrote a book report, he got an A+.

AS THE CROW FLIES

THIS WAY

MEANING: A distance that is measured **as the crow flies** is measured as a straight line between two points.

ORIGIN: This phrase uses the idea that crows can fly directly from point to point without going around obstacles.

EXAMPLE: June's cousin lived only a few miles away **as the crow flies**, but the winding roads made the drive there take a long time.

READ THE RIOT ACT

MEANING: To **read the riot act** to someone is to scold them harshly.

ORIGIN: This phrase comes from a British law passed in 1715. The law said that crowds had to break up if the law was read out loud.

EXAMPLE: The teacher **read the riot act** to his students because they wouldn't stop throwing paper airplanes.

KANGAROO COURT

MEANING: A **kangaroo court** is a court that is unfair.

ORIGIN: The exact origin of this phrase is unknown. It might have come from the American West in the 1850s. Informal courts were set up in new parts of the country. People may have called them kangaroo courts because kangaroos were strange or unnatural to them.

EXAMPLE: Everybody knew it was a **kangaroo court**. Even though Mika didn't steal the pack of gum, the judge was still going to find her guilty.

TO MAKE HAY WHILE THE SUN SHINES

MEANING: To make hay while the sun shines is to take advantage of opportunities while you can.

ORIGIN: This phrase comes from farmers. They have to gather their hay right away when the weather is sunny.

EXAMPLE: Elijah's favorite series of books was on sale. He decided **to make hay while the sun shines** and bought all three at once.

THINK TANK

MEANING: A **think tank** is a group of experts who meet to solve problems.

ORIGIN: This phrase originally just meant "brain." It later meant a room where problems were solved. It gained its modern meaning around 1950.

EXAMPLE: The **think tank** held an emergency meeting to discuss the waffle shortage.

MAGIC BULLET

MEANING: A **magic bullet** is a quick and simple solution, usually to an illness.

ORIGIN: In 1906, German scientist Paul Ehrlich used the German word *Zauberkugel* in this way. This was translated to "magic bullet" in English.

EXAMPLE: Angelica found that drinking orange juice was not a **magic bullet** for curing her cold.

THE CARDS ARE STACKED AGAINST ME

MEANING: When **the cards are stacked against you**, a situation is to your disadvantage.

ORIGIN: The phrase comes from card games. A cheating player arranges the cards in a way that helps him or her and hurts you.

EXAMPLE: The cards were stacked against Mike. He had an hour to mow the lawn, clean his room, and do his homework or he couldn't go to the concert.

IN A NUTSHELL

MEANING: Something that is **in a nutshell** is said in a short and simplified way.

ORIGIN: This phrase was used by Shakespeare in his play *Hamlet*. It comes from the common use of a nutshell to represent a small space.

EXAMPLE: Gerald was very good at basketball, tennis, and jump rope. **In a nutshell**, he was a great athlete.

AS HAPPY AS A CLAM

MEANING: Someone who is **as happy as a clam** is very happy.

ORIGIN: This idiom is shortened from its original version: happy as a clam at high water. High water makes clams happy because they need water to live. It came from the East Coast of the United States, where clams are common.

EXAMPLE: Marcus was **as happy as a clam**. His mother had bought him a shiny new stapler.

CLEAN SOMEONE'S CLOCK

MEANING: To **clean someone's clock** is to defeat them.

ORIGIN: The phrase originally meant to punch a person in the face. "Clean" meant to beat someone. "Clock" refers to the "face" of a clock. The meaning later changed to mean defeat in general.

EXAMPLE: Stephanie **cleaned Fernando's clock** in the chess match. She didn't lose a single piece.

DYED IN THE WOOL

MEANING: A person who is **dyed in the wool** never changes his or her opinions.

ORIGIN: The meaning comes from dyeing sheep's wool. When it is dyed right away, the color is more permanent.

EXAMPLE: Ash was a **dyed-in-the-wool** fan of his high school's football team.

RULE OF THUMB

MEANING: A **rule of thumb** is a general rule.

ORIGIN: This phrase probably comes from the time when body parts were used to measure things. The name of one of these measurements is still used today, the foot.

EXAMPLE: Alma had a good **rule of thumb**. She could watch television for thirty minutes for every hour she spent on homework.

THE COAST IS CLEAR

MEANING: When **the coast is clear**, a risk or threat is gone.

ORIGIN: The phrase once referred to smugglers, people who brought goods into a country illegally. Smugglers needed to land their ships on the coast secretly.

EXAMPLE: The coast was clear! Dot's mom had left the house, so Dot could wrap her birthday presents.

PASS WITH FLYING COLORS

MEANING: To **pass something with flying colors** is to succeed at it completely.

ORIGIN: The phrase refers to an army or navy waving flags after winning a battle.

EXAMPLE: Sven **passed with flying colors**. His remote-control blimp flew faster and higher than anyone else's.

CLOSE, BUT NO CIGAR

MEANING: An effort that is **close, but no cigar** is almost successful but has no reward.

ORIGIN: This phrase likely came from games at fairgrounds many years ago. A common prize for winning these games was a cigar.

EXAMPLE: "**Close, but no cigar**," the spelling bee judge said to Bruce. "You forgot the silent *t*."

FROM SOUP TO NUTS

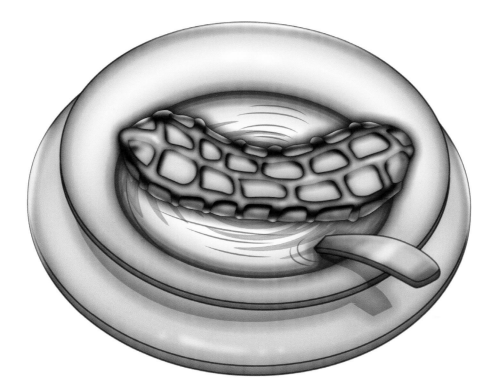

MEANING: From soup to nuts means "the whole thing."

ORIGIN: This phrase comes from a traditional meal that begins with a soup and ends with nuts for dessert.

EXAMPLE: Terri read every book in the school library **from soup to nuts**.

PENCIL PUSHER

MEANING: Pencil pusher is a rude name for someone who works in an office.

ORIGIN: The idiom comes from the use of pencils in office work. It is meant to contrast that work with more physical labor.

EXAMPLE: Suzanna the plumber called Troy the accountant a **pencil pusher**. He broke his sink while trying to fix his faucet.

BURN THE CANDLE AT BOTH ENDS

MEANING: To **burn the candle at both ends** is to tire yourself out by working hard.

ORIGIN: The phrase comes from lighting both ends of a candle. This produces a brighter light but also uses up the candle more quickly.

EXAMPLE: Daphne **burned the candle at both ends** staying up late and getting up early to work on her science fair project.

STEALING SOMEONE'S THUNDER

MEANING: When you **steal someone's thunder**, you use their idea or invention to your own advantage.

ORIGIN: In the 1700s, an actor invented a way to make thunder noises for stage plays. When he heard his noise at a different play, he complained that they had stolen his thunder.

EXAMPLE: Rosa felt that Kirk had **stolen her thunder**. The day after she brought the principal an apple, he brought a whole fruit basket.

AT THE DROP OF A HAT

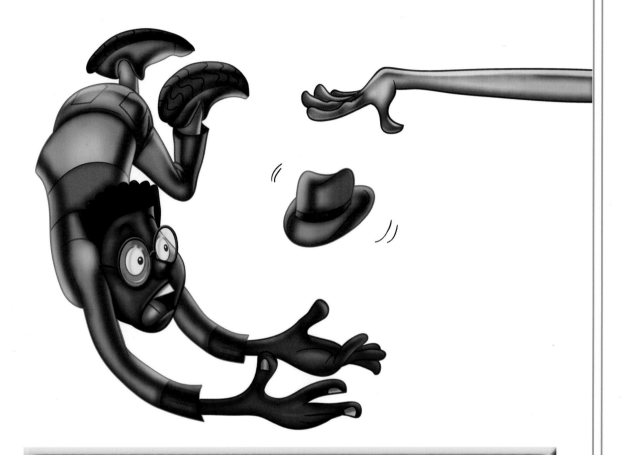

MEANING: Something done **at the drop of a hat** is done suddenly.

ORIGIN: This phrase may come from the practice of dropping a hat to start a competition.

EXAMPLE: Jacquelyn stopped what she was doing **at the drop of a hat** whenever she remembered her favorite television show was on.

About the Author

Arnold Ringstad lives in Minneapolis, where he graduated from the University of Minnesota in 2011. He enjoys reading books about space exploration and playing board games with his girlfriend. Writing about idioms makes him as happy as a clam.

About the Illustrator

Dan McGeehan loves being an illustrator. His art appears in many magazines and children's books. He currently lives in Oklahoma.